For

The EIGHT NIGHTS of Hanukah

By Suzanne Beilenson and
Rabbi Daniel S. Wolk

Illustrations by James Henry

PETER PAUPER PRESS, INC.
WHITE PLAINS · NEW YORK

For Johanna Loeb

Rock of Ages words appear in
Gates of Prayer © CCAR 1975.
Used by permission.

Copyright © 1993
Peter Pauper Press, Inc.
202 Mamaroneck Avenue
White Plains, NY 10601
All rights reserved
ISBN 0-88088-781-8
Printed in Hong Kong
7   6

The Eight
Nights of
Hanukah

The First Night:

A Little History of Hanukah

*J*ewish families all around the world come together in the winter of each year to celebrate the holiday of Hanukah. Hanukah is truly a time of celebration, for the holiday recalls a momentous event—an uprising in the name of religious freedom.

The story of this uprising began in 168 B.C.E. when the land of Israel came under the control of the Greco-Syrian Empire. Antiochus, the emperor, outlawed the practice of Judaism, in his attempt to force all people to worship the pagan gods of Hellenism. The Greco-Syrians desecrated the Temple in Jerusalem, and they commanded the Jews to eat

pork as proof of their allegiance to Antiochus.

Eventually, Antiochus' men came to a village in Judea named Modi'in. A Greco-Syrian soldier entered the Temple and started to sacrifice a pig on the altar. Enraged by this action, an old priest named Mattathias the Hasmonean stabbed the soldier to death. A revolt had begun!

Pursued by the Greco-Syrians, Mattathias and his five sons, known as the Maccabees, fled to the hills surrounding Jerusalem. There, the resistance movement took form. Before Mattathias died, he selected his son, Judah the Hammer, to lead the fight. And Judah did so valiantly. Through strategy and foresight, the rebels overcame all of Antiochus'

forces, including an army
riding elephants!

In victory, the Maccabees
liberated Jerusalem from the
invaders, and on the 25th day
of Kislev they cleansed the
Temple, which had been
defiled. Hanukah, which
means dedication, commem-
orates that day.

According to legend, a

miracle then occurred. To
rededicate the Temple, holy
oil was needed to light the
Temple's great menorah, or
candelabrum. The Jews
searched and searched, but
found only one small cruse of
sacramental oil, barely enough
to last a day. Knowing it
would take eight days to
prepare new holy oil, they

nevertheless used the little bit
of oil and lit the menorah.
Miraculously, the oil burned
for eight days!

The Second Night:

Hanukah Lights

*I*n celebrating the festival
of Hanukah, the menorah is a
symbol of the miracle of the
oil. While the traditional
Temple menorah has seven
branches, the Hanukah
menorah has nine. Eight
branches signify the eight
days the oil burned in the

Temple, and the ninth branch, known as the *shammas* or servant, holds the light from which the other eight are kindled.

Other explanations of the Hanukah menorah have been offered. For example, some people believe that when the Jews went to cleanse the Temple, it was too dark inside to see, but they found eight

iron Greco-Syrian spears. They
lined up the spears, and
burned a candle atop each
one to light their work.

Regardless of its origins, the
Hanukah menorah forever
signifies truth, light, and life.
For this reason, the menorah
is placed either in the
doorway or the window of a
Jewish home. Lit at sunset, the
lights of the menorah are for

all to see and to remember
the Jewish love of freedom.
And because this symbol is so
precious, the lights of the
menorah are sacred and are
not to be used for any
practical purpose. There must
always be at least one other
lamp lit to illuminate the
home.

The first known Hanukah
menorahs were made of clay,

and used oil and wicks. As
time went on, the designs
became much more intricate,
and materials such as pewter,
silver, brass, glass, and stone
were used. Many menorahs
are standing; some are
constructed to hang on the
wall. Today, candles of
different colors are often used,
but a menorah can easily be
created by setting nine small

pots, filled with olive oil, in a row (but remember to set the *shammas* apart!), and by dropping a piece of string in each one as a wick.

The correct procedure for lighting the menorah has been hotly contested for centuries. One main school of thought, following Bet Shammai, contends that all eight lights should be burned

the first night, and a light
should be taken away each
night following. Reducing the
lights signifies the days still to
come. However, most people
follow the method taught by
Bet Hillel. The school of Hillel
argues that only one candle
should be kindled the first
night, with a candle added on
each successive night to
symbolize increasing light and

joy. The candles should be placed in the menorah from right to left but lit from left to right.

The *shammas* should be lit first. Then, while the blessings are recited, the *shammas* is used to kindle each light. (If the menorah sits in the window, the menorah may be reversed after it is lit so that passers-by view the lights in

the correct position.)

The Talmud commands that there be one light for each man and his family. Some families interpret this to mean one menorah only; others light one menorah for each family member. The Sephardic tradition goes even further. Instead of adding one light for each night of the holiday, a whole menorah is added!

No matter how the menorah is lit, the lights of Hanukah are a sign of the Jewish people, the heroes of the Hanukah story, and the brightness of the future.

The Third
Night:

Prayers and Songs of Hanukah

*A*fter lighting the *shammas* and as the other candles are kindled, the following blessings are pronounced:

Blessed is the Lord our God, Ruler of the Universe, who

hallows us with His Mitzvot,
and commands us to kindle
the Hanukah lights.

Blessed is the Lord our God,
Ruler of the Universe, who
performed wondrous deeds for
our ancestors in days of old,
at this season.

(On the first night only, the
following blessing is also
recited:)

Blessed is the Lord our God,
Ruler of the Universe, for
granting us life, for sustaining
us, and for enabling us to
reach this season.

After the lights are kindled,
many families also follow the
custom of singing *Rock of Ages*
or in Hebrew, *Maoz Tzur.*

Rock of Ages let our song
Praise Your saving power;

You, amid the raging foes,
Were our sheltering tower.
Furious they assailed us,
But Your arm availed us,
   And Your word
   Broke their sword
When our own strength
failed us.
(repeat last three lines)

Kindling new the holy lamps,
Priests approved in suffering,
Purified the nation's shrine,

Brought to God their offering.
And His courts surrounding
Hear, in joy abounding,
  Happy throngs
  Singing songs,
With a mighty sounding.
(repeat last three lines)

Children of the Maccabees,
Whether free or fettered,
Wake the echoes of the songs,
Where you may be scattered.

Yours the message cheering
That the time is nearing
   Which will see
   All men free,
Tyrants disappearing.
(repeat last three lines)

Adapted from Gustav Gottheil
and M. Jastrow

The Fourth Night:

Hanukah in Israel

While the festival of
Hanukah in the United States
is a celebration shared by
family and friends, in Israel it
is a full affair of state. The
menorah, which is an emblem
of the State of Israel, can be
seen everywhere from the top
of Masada to local shop

windows. The largest menorahs anywhere (albeit, electric!) can be found in Israel, and they cast their light from the tops of water towers and public buildings. Some public menorahs are lit using oil-soaked cloth, rather than oil or candles.

Traditionally, schools are closed throughout the eight days, no doubt contributing to

children's love of Hanukah.
On the 25th day of Kislev,
children dressed in white and
carrying lighted candles fill the
streets of Tel Aviv. Songs are
sung, and there is dancing in
the streets with the Scrolls of
the Law.

Parades, games, and feasts
are also a large part of the
Israeli Hanukah. Even a torch
relay takes place. Starting in

the Maccabees' home town of
Modi'in, a torch is lit and
carried by a runner. After
about a mile, the torch is
passed to another runner. The
relay continues all the way to
Jerusalem where the Israeli
president kindles a great
menorah with the torch flame.
This event, which replays the
Maccabees' march toward

freedom, symbolizes the connection between today's Jews and their victorious past.

להדליכ נר דינוכה

The Fifth
Night:

The Dreidel and Other Hanukah Fun

$\mathcal{O}$ f all the games children play during Hanukah, the dreidel game is the most popular.

The dreidel is simply a four-sided top with a different Hebrew letter inscribed on each side. The four letters,

nun, gimmel, heh, and *shin*
stand for the Hebrew phrase,
Neis gadol hayah sham, which
translates into "A great miracle
happened there." The miracle,
of course, is the miracle of the
oil. Interestingly, Israeli dreidels
replace the fourth letter *shin*
with *peh. Peh* stands for the
Hebrew word *poh,* meaning
"here" in English. The phrase
then becomes "A great miracle
happened *here.*"

To play the dreidel game, every participant has to contribute a coin to the pot at the start of each round. Then each player spins the dreidel. If the dreidel falls with the letter *nun* upright, he or she neither wins nor loses. *Gimmel* wins the entire pot; *heh* wins half the pot; and *shin* or *peh* means the player must throw another coin into the pot.

Although games of chance are not normally favored, an exception is made for Hanukah. Legend has it that at the time of the Maccabees (and also in Germany in a later age), the Jews used the dreidel game to mask their study of Torah which had been prohibited by Antiochus. If any of the authorities came upon them studying, they would start

spinning the dreidel as if they were gambling, thereby fooling the Greco-Syrians!

Besides the dreidel, children are often given Hanukah *gelt,* or money. Sometimes it may be real coins, at other times simply gold-foiled chocolate. To show that they were a free people, the Maccabees had struck coins when they liberated Jerusalem. Hanukah

gelt is thus a sign of freedom.

During the Hanukah festival, students and adults play riddles called *ketowes*. These riddles are a type of mathematical puzzle to which the solution is always 44, or the total number of candles which are lit during Hanukah. There are also riddles involving wordplay, acronyms, and anagrams. One of the best-

known of these riddles is
"Why do we call this holiday
Hanukah?" The answer can be
found by breaking the word
Hanukah into two smaller
words. *Hanu* means "they
rested," and *kah* means "25."
Together, it becomes "They
rested on the 25th day."
Indeed, the Maccabees rested
after their battle on the 25th
day of Kislev, and rededicated
the Temple.

Another famous riddle is "Why was Judah called Maccabee?" The answer comes from Judah's battle cry, *"Mi Kamoka Baelim Adonai!"* which translates into "Who is Like Thee Among their gods, O Lord!" In Hebrew, the first letter of each word—MKBI— spells Maccabee!

*The Sixth
Night:*

Hanukah and the Artist

*T*he story of Hanukah inspires all Jews, but it especially stimulates the creative spirit in artists, both Jewish and non-Jewish.

In 1747, the composer George Frederick Handel wrote an oratorio entitled *Judah Maccabeus* for the

Prince of Wales. The Prince had commissioned a piece from Handel, stating that he wanted to honor the Duke of Cumberland, who had led the English military to victory in Scotland. Handel's choice of Judah Maccabee as a theme seemed highly appropriate to commemorate another noble leader.

In the 1800's, the American poet and Harvard professor,

Henry Wadsworth Longfellow,
was also inspired by the
Maccabee story. His five-act
play, *Judah Maccabeus,* retells
the struggle of the Jewish
people against the Hellenist
Syrians.

Short stories and poetry,
using the Hanukah theme,
also abound. Emma Lazarus,
one of the best-known Jewish
poets, authored many such
verses. The following poem

(from *The Feast of Lights*) is only one example of her work:

*K*indle the taper like the steadfast star

　Ablaze on evening's forehead o'er

　the earth,

And add each night a luster till afar

An eightfold splendor shine above
thy hearth.

Clash, Israel, the cymbals, touch the lyre,

Blow the brass trumpet and the

harsh-tongued horn;

Chant psalms of victory till the heart
takes fire,

The Maccabean spirit leap newborn.

The Seventh Night:

The Feast of Hanukah

*D*uring Hanukah, there are often big meals to celebrate. Indeed, fasting is forbidden during the eight days. Dairy products, especially cheese delicacies, are often eaten. This custom is associated with the story of Judith,

who saved a Jewish city from the invading Assyrians by plying their general, Holofernes, with cheese and wine until he became very drunk. When Holofernes fell asleep, she cut off his head, and thereby saved her city.

Latkes, or potato pancakes, are perhaps the most popular dish during the holiday. The latkes are made of matzoh

meal or potatoes and are then
fried in oil—recalling the
miracle of the oil! Therefore,
any foods fried in oils are very
appropriate at this time,
which explains why in Israel,
yeast-raised jelly doughnuts
are also widely eaten.
(Ready ingredients before
making potato latkes. If grated
potatoes are left standing they
will turn brown.)

POTATO LATKES

4 large potatoes, grated
3 tablespoons matzoh meal
3 eggs, beaten
1 teaspoon salt
⅛ teaspoon finely ground
  pepper
1 teaspoon onion powder
Vegetable oil for frying

Grate the potatoes, and
squeeze out as much water as

possible. Mix the grated potatoes, matzoh meal, eggs, salt, pepper, and onion powder. Heat oil in a frying pan. When the oil is hot, drop the potato mixture by tablespoons into the oil, and drain on paper toweling.

The pancakes may be fried in advance and frozen. Before serving, lay the pancakes in one layer on a foil-lined

cookie sheet and reheat in a
375° oven for about 20
minutes. Serve with applesauce.
6 servings.

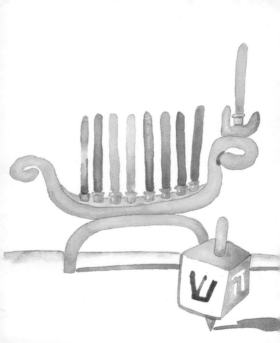

The Eighth
Night:

The Mitzvot

*T*here are six *mitzvot,* or religious practices, of Hanukah which should be remembered and performed.

Each person should have his or her own menorah at Hanukah.

*Each individual should kindle
the Hanukah lights each
evening during the eight days
of the festival.*

*The whole family should
actively participate in the
lighting of the Hanukah
menorah.*

*Each person or family should
share the lighting of the*

menorah and the meaning of
the Hanukah festival with
friends and neighbors.

Each person should give to
charity or perform volunteer
service during the eight days of
Hanukah.

Parents should relate the story
of Hanukah to their children.

*A*nd once the gift-giving and present-opening is complete, and the children have settled down, it would surely be a *mitzvah* to read to them the poem, *Eight Little Candles,* by Jessie E. Sampter:

EIGHT LITTLE CANDLES

I thought of all the wondrous

things the Maccabees had done;

I lit a little candle—

And then there was one.

I thought of all the wondrous

things that I myself might do;

And lit another candle—

And then there were two.

I thought of Eretz Yisrael, the

Maccabees, and me;

I lit another candle—

And then there were three.

I thought of Jewish heroes that

fell in peace and war;

And lit another candle—

And then there were four.

I thought of young Judeans all

pledged to serve and strive;

I lit another candle—

And then there were five.

I thought of Jewish pioneers

with shovels, rakes, and picks;

And lit another candle—

And then there were six.

I thought of white as white as

stars, of blue as blue as heaven;

I lit another candle—

And then there were seven.

I thought of the great Lord our

God who guides us early and

late;

And lit another candle—

And then there were eight.